THE DAILY NUDGE
VOLUME ONE

WHEN DID YOU FIRST NOTICE

BECA LEWIS

PERCEPTION PUBLISHING

All rights reserved. No part of this book may be reproduced or transmitted in any form or by any means, electronic or mechanical, including photocopying, recording, or by any information storage and retrieval system, without written permission from the author, except for the inclusion of brief quotations in a review.

Copyright ©2022 Beca Lewis

Contents

Using The Daily Nudge	IV
The Daily Nudge Volume One	1
In The Area Of Ourselves	3
In The Area Of Communication	29
In The Area Of Love	55
In The Area Of Money	81
Other Daily Nudge Volumes	107
Author Note	109
Also By Beca	111
About Beca	114

Using The Daily Nudge

How you use this *Daily Nudge* is up to you. My intent is that you use it as something that sparks a new way to see the world, and that opens up new possibilities.

Perhaps read a Nudge daily, and then use the note section to write what it meant to you, what you think, what's going on with you. It's yours to use as you desire. And each day may be different. In fact, for sure it will be, since you will be.

However you use it, make it work for you. It's your *Daily Nudge*, after all.

And if you find it useful, perhaps share how it has helped you.

Shifting with you, Beca

THE DAILY NUDGE VOLUME ONE

- Ourselves
- Communication
- Love
- Money

IN THE AREA OF OURSELVES

Since *What You Perceive To Be Reality Magnifies*, imagine the outcome of taking **just 30 seconds a day** to become more aware and then consciously choosing what you are going to focus on for the day.

When Did You First Notice That: [1]

What you experience in life is a direct result of how you define yourself.

TODAY'S STATEMENT:

I define myself as the compound idea of God, Infinite Intelligence.

Notes:

When Did You First Notice That: [2]

You are not at all who you thought you were, but you are everything you were afraid you might be, and isn't that wonderful!

TODAY'S STATEMENT:

I celebrate all that I Am.

Notes:

When Did You First Notice That: [3]

We are tempted to eat more when the food is free, or when we have paid too much for it.

TODAY'S STATEMENT:

I am not tempted by what I don't need.

Notes:

When Did You First Notice That: [4]

Helping someone else in need can lift depression.

TODAY'S STATEMENT:

Today I practice lifting.

Notes:

When Did You First Notice That: [5]

If you don't clearly state what you want, you will probably never get it. This is true for intents in life as well as things you want from the store.

TODAY'S STATEMENT:

I clearly state my intents!

Notes:

When Did You First Notice That: [6]

No one can read your mind, because you are the only one in there.

TODAY'S STATEMENT:

Today I share my heart by kindly and clearly speaking what is going on in my mind.

Notes:

When Did You First Notice That: 7

People often say "Oh I shouldn't" as they reach for their "forbidden" food.

TODAY'S STATEMENT:

There is no forbidden food, just forbidden words.

Notes:

When Did You First Notice That: [8]

No matter how many people's lives you change, it is yours that you live in.

TODAY'S STATEMENT:

I will begin at home within my own life and within my own heart.

Notes:

When Did You First Notice That: [9]

Uncontrolled emotion is your worst enemy.

TODAY'S STATEMENT:

I exchange emotion for feelings that come from Truth.

Notes:

When Did You First Notice That: [10]

The world and all its contents are a mirror of what we believe to be true.

TODAY'S STATEMENT:

I consciously choose what I want the mirror to reflect.

Notes:

When Did You First Notice That: [11]

When you lie to yourself, everything you do stems from a lie.

TODAY'S STATEMENT:

I trust myself.

Notes:

When Did You First Notice That: [12]

When you lie to yourself, everything you do stems from a lie.

TODAY'S STATEMENT:

I trust myself.

Notes:

When Did You First Notice That: [13]

It's easier to remember all the "right" reasons why something can't be done than imagine how it can.

TODAY'S STATEMENT:

I love to imagine beyond the possible.

Notes:

When Did You First Notice That: [14]

The more we dislike ourselves for who we have become, the less likely it is that we will become anything else.

TODAY'S STATEMENT:

Who I have become is glorious.

Notes:

When Did You First Notice That: [15]

When we are on fire with what we can accomplish, we must be careful not to be distracted or someone may put the fire out.

TODAY'S STATEMENT:

I am not distracted.

Notes:

When Did You First Notice That: [16]

If we criticized others the way we criticize ourselves, the effect would be devastating.

TODAY'S STATEMENT:

Criticism is no longer welcome in my thinking.

Notes:

When Did You First Notice That: [17]
☐ ☐ ☐ ☐

It is easy to see what other people are doing wrong, especially if we have done the same thing ourselves.☐

TODAY'S STATEMENT:

I reap the benefits of the wisdom I have gained.

Notes:

When Did You First Notice That: [18]

The longer we wait to do, have, or be, the more weight we carry, and the harder it is to move it.

TODAY'S STATEMENT:

I take action, no matter how small, toward the joys in my life.

Notes:

When Did You First Notice That: [19]

We can not live our life by proxy.

TODAY'S STATEMENT:

I celebrate the living of my life.

Notes:

When Did You First Notice That: 20

What other people say to us about us is usually what we already know.

TODAY'S STATEMENT:

I use the mirror of others to dissolve what isn't true while living in Truth.

Notes:

When Did You First Notice That: [21]

If you lie to yourself enough, you will soon believe the lie.

TODAY'S STATEMENT:

I choose to never lie to myself again.

Notes:

When Did You First Notice That: [22]

People who say they don't care what other people think about them are the ones who care the most.

TODAY'S STATEMENT:

I decide what is best for my life.

Notes:

When Did You First Notice That: [23]

It is dangerous to attach the ego to anything volatile.

TODAY'S STATEMENT:

I am giving up the danger of ego and attachment.

Notes:

When Did You First Notice That: 24

When other people say something nice about us, it's hard to believe they are talking about us.

TODAY'S STATEMENT:

I do not separate myself from good.

Notes:

When Did You First Notice That: [25]

If you are content, you will not change. If you are at peace, you are willing to change.

TODAY'S STATEMENT:

I am at peace, and I am willing.

Notes:

IN THE AREA OF COMMUNICATION

Since *What You Perceive To Be Reality Magnifies*, imagine the outcome of taking **just 30 seconds a day** to become more aware and then consciously choosing what you are going to focus on for the day.

When Did You First Notice That: [26]

In a lecture, class, or seminar, there is always someone in the group who will ask exactly the same question that the teacher just answered.

TODAY'S STATEMENT:

I listen!

Notes:

When Did You First Notice That: [27]

Ignoring a problem does not make it go away.

TODAY'S STATEMENT:

I face any problem knowing there is a solution that blesses everyone.

Notes:

When Did You First Notice That: [28]

To communicate effectively, you must step outside yourself and become the person to whom you are communicating.

TODAY'S STATEMENT:

I am willing to be heard.

Notes:

When Did You First Notice That: [29]

There will always be someone who will misinterpret what you say, so you might as well say what you want to say

TODAY'S STATEMENT:

I am not afraid to speak.

Notes:

When Did You First Notice That: [30]

In the long run, it is easier to tell the truth than to remember the lie.

TODAY'S STATEMENT:

I take the easy way and tell the truth.

Notes:

When Did You First Notice That: 31

If you want to be understood by someone else, you must speak in their language, not yours.

TODAY'S STATEMENT:

My intent is to be understood.

Notes:

When Did You First Notice That: 32

A smile says the same thing in any language.

TODAY'S STATEMENT:

I love to smile!

Notes:

When Did You First Notice That:[33]

One unkind spoken word acts like a hole in the dike.

TODAY'S STATEMENT:

If an unkind word escapes, I immediately stop the flow.

Notes:

When Did You First Notice That: [34]

Words are not enough.

TODAY'S STATEMENT:

I take action on what I feel.

Notes:

When Did You First Notice That:[35]

The first person you need to communicate to is yourself.

TODAY'S STATEMENT:

I pay attention to myself.

Notes:

When Did You First Notice That: [36]

Some people communicate by not doing what is asked of them.

TODAY'S STATEMENT:

I pay attention to myself.

Notes:

When Did You First Notice That: [37]

No often means maybe.

TODAY'S STATEMENT:

I listen for the real meaning behind what is being said.

Notes:

When Did You First Notice That: [38]

What you do is more important than how well you say what you will do.

TODAY'S STATEMENT:

My actions speak louder than my words.

Notes:

When Did You First Notice That: [39]

Words have only the value we assign to them.

TODAY'S STATEMENT:

I listen for the true meaning behind each word.

Notes:

When Did You First Notice That: [40]

When we speak, it is like playing "whisper down the alley." What comes back to us bears little resemblance to what we have said.

TODAY'S STATEMENT:

I go to the source.

Notes:

When Did You First Notice That: [41]

People prefer to believe what they hear about another, rather than asking the person themselves for the truth.

TODAY'S STATEMENT:

I ask directly and listen for Truth.

Notes:

When Did You First Notice That: [42]

If we want to hear what the other person is really saying, we have to stop comparing it with what we already know.

TODAY'S STATEMENT:

I am willing to step outside of what I think I know.

Notes:

When Did You First Notice That: [43]

Communication is the response that we get.

TODAY'S STATEMENT:

I observe responses and adjust my communication accordingly.

Notes:

When Did You First Notice That: [44]

Some people talk to fill up the silence.

TODAY'S STATEMENT:

Silence is my friend.

Notes:

When Did You First Notice That: [45]

Communication needs a listener.

TODAY'S STATEMENT:

Listening brings me joy.

Notes:

When Did You First Notice That: [46]

Communication is the response that we get.

TODAY'S STATEMENT:

I observe responses and adjust my communication accordingly.

Notes:

# When Did You First Notice That: [47]

Communication is the response that we get.

TODAY'S STATEMENT:

I observe responses and adjust my communication accordingly.

Notes:

When Did You First Notice That: [48]

It is dangerous to assume that communication has taken place.

TODAY'S STATEMENT:

Observing actions after communicating tells me what has been heard.

Notes:

When Did You First Notice That: [49]

Extra words do not make better communication.

TODAY'S STATEMENT:

I *don't need extra words when I speak from my heart.*

Notes:

When Did You First Notice That: [50]

When communication comes too late, it is no longer communication. It is old news.

TODAY'S STATEMENT:

I do not withhold what must be said.

Notes:

IN THE AREA OF LOVE

Since *What You Perceive To Be Reality Magnifies*, imagine the outcome of taking **just 30 seconds a day** to become more aware and then consciously choosing what you are going to focus on for the day.

When Did You First Notice That: 51

You sometimes feel that you can only be somebody if somebody else loves you, so you give up who you are so you can be loved.

TODAY'S STATEMENT:

I love myself first so that I never have to give up who I am to be loved.

Notes:

When Did You First Notice That: [52]

When you are afraid of commitment, what you may be afraid of is the other person's lack of commitment.

TODAY'S STATEMENT:

I commit to myself first, and as in all things begun from within, all else follows for good without my needing to control it.

Notes:

When Did You First Notice That: [53]

Respect and admiration are the basis for enduring true love.

TODAY'S STATEMENT:

I focus on what I respect and admire about the people I love.

Notes:

When Did You First Notice That: [54]

Without awareness and acceptance of your True unique self, you may live your life, either having someone and being "nobody", or being somebody and having no one.

TODAY'S STATEMENT:

I am aware of and accept my True unique self.

Notes:

When Did You First Notice That: [55]

When you are trying as hard as you can to be everything to someone, it won't ever be enough, because you are trying instead of being.

TODAY'S STATEMENT:

I celebrate the being that I am.

Notes:

When Did You First Notice That: 56

It is sometimes not the person you are in love with, it is the feeling.

TODAY'S STATEMENT:

I know that the feeling of Love is ever-present.

Notes:

When Did You First Notice That:

Loving each other does not guarantee that each will be understood, or will understand.

TODAY'S STATEMENT:

I take the time to understand the people that I love.

Notes:

When Did You First Notice That: [58]

Love is an art that must be practiced, but it takes two to be in a loving relationship.

TODAY'S STATEMENT:

I practice the art of Love for Love's sake.

Notes:

When Did You First Notice That: [59]

People marry for many reasons, often disguised as love.

TODAY'S STATEMENT:

I begin and end with Love.

Notes:

When Did You First Notice That: [60]

True love is more precious than diamonds, more fragile than a rose, and as tough as steel.

TODAY'S STATEMENT:

True Love is who I Am.

Notes:

When Did You First Notice That: [61]

Surrendering to love takes courage.

TODAY'S STATEMENT:

I rest in the awareness that Love supports and guides me.

Notes:

When Did You First Notice That: [62]

If we want to receive love, first we must unconditionally give love.

TODAY'S STATEMENT:

I love without judgment or need for approval.

Notes:

When Did You First Notice That: [63]

Prince Charming and The Princess are really you.

TODAY'S STATEMENT:

I am not waiting for love as it is here as me now.

Notes:

When Did You First Notice That: [64]

The happier one is, the more love they are willing to feel.

TODAY'S STATEMENT:

I will begin by deciding to be happy now.

Notes:

When Did You First Notice That: [65]

Real love sets people free.

TODAY'S STATEMENT:

The more I love, the more freedom I have and give.

Notes:

When Did You First Notice That: [66]

Love is always available. However, it is often missed because it doesn't look like the love in the movies.

TODAY'S STATEMENT:

I see and accept love in all its forms available for me now.

Notes:

When Did You First Notice That: [67]

If you feel that you will love someone more when they become more of what you want, you do not love them.

TODAY'S STATEMENT:

I do not change people; I see them as God sees them.

Notes:

When Did You First Notice That: [68]

Love requires total commitment.

TODAY'S STATEMENT:

I commit to Love.

Notes:

When Did You First Notice That: [69]

Holidays distort the meaning of love in order to profit from the public's desire to prove to themselves that someone cares.

TODAY'S STATEMENT:

I know that am I always cared for by others, and they always know I care about them.

Notes:

When Did You First Notice That: 70

If you accept someone else's interpretation of love as your reality, you will be unhappy.

TODAY'S STATEMENT:

I accept the Infinite Principle of Love as my Reality.

Notes:

When Did You First Notice That: [71]

You can often tell how much another person loves and respects you by the choices they make that affect you.

TODAY'S STATEMENT:

I notice and adjust my choices based on my love for others.

Notes:

When Did You First Notice That: [72]

When women talk about wanting romance, what they want is time and attention.

TODAY'S STATEMENT:

Love is timeless and ever attentive.

Notes:

When Did You First Notice That: [73]

Love expands-hate contracts.

TODAY'S STATEMENT:

I expand.

Notes:

When Did You First Notice That: 74

We show others how much we love them the way we want to be shown. This may not be the way they understand it.

TODAY'S STATEMENT:

I act from the love needs of those I love.

Notes:

When Did You First Notice That: [75]

Love is a series of small acts of kindness.

TODAY'S STATEMENT:

I find joy in being excessively kind.

Notes:

IN THE AREA OF MONEY

Since *What You Perceive To Be Reality Magnifies*, imagine the outcome of taking **just 30 seconds a day** to become more aware and then consciously choosing what you are going to focus on for the day.

When Did You First Notice That: [76]

Gratitude is the key that opens the door to all riches.

TODAY'S STATEMENT:

My gratitude consistently overflows.

Notes:

When Did You First Notice That: 77

If you are not careful, what you own, owns you.

TODAY'S STATEMENT:

I let go of what I don't need.

Notes:

When Did You First Notice That: [78]

Money is emotion, not logic.

TODAY'S STATEMENT:

The Principle of abundance guides me.

Notes:

When Did You First Notice That: [79]

The worldview game of lack breeds greed.

TODAY'S STATEMENT:

I am not playing the game of lack.

Notes:

When Did You First Notice That: [80]

Both wealth and poverty are first a point of view and a state of mind.

TODAY'S STATEMENT:

My point of view is infinite abundance and my state of mind is gratitude.

Notes:

When Did You First Notice That: [81]

Wealth can not buy grace, but grace is wealth.

TODAY'S STATEMENT:

Grace is what I Am.

Notes:

When Did You First Notice That: [82]

We let other people's definition of wealth become our own.

TODAY'S STATEMENT:

I have a deep understanding of living wealth.

Notes:

When Did You First Notice That: [83]

Debt is a gamble that the future will be better than the present.

TODAY'S STATEMENT:

I am aware that all I need is present now.

Notes:

When Did You First Notice That: [84]

Ships can not come in if they are never sent out.

TODAY'S STATEMENT:

I constantly and consistently launch my ships filled with what I have to offer.

Notes:

When Did You First Notice That: 85

We often work so hard for money that we lose sight of the fact that we are really working to provide for the ones we love. In the process, we may lose the ones we love.

TODAY'S STATEMENT:

By being completely present, I am provision.

Notes:

When Did You First Notice That: [86]

Money is one of the multitudes of symbols of understanding wealth, not the cause.

TODAY'S STATEMENT:

I begin my awareness of wealth from within.

Notes:

When Did You First Notice That: [87]

Money is a symbol of an exchange and sharing of services and gifts; nothing more.

TODAY'S STATEMENT:

I love to participate in the exchange and sharing of services and gifts.

Notes:

When Did You First Notice That: [88]

For many people, it is harder to talk about money than it is to talk about sex.

TODAY'S STATEMENT:

I don't take the idea of money personally.

Notes:

When Did You First Notice That: [89]

Most people spend their entire life working for money, not understanding how money can work for them.

TODAY'S STATEMENT:

I am willing to learn how money works.

Notes:

When Did You First Notice That: [90]

If you think that an ATM receipt tells you how much money you have in the bank, you are living in a delusion.

TODAY'S STATEMENT:

I am consistently aware.

Notes:

When Did You First Notice That: [91]

Telling people how poor or broke you are so that you will fit in, will not motivate them to see you as wealthy.

TODAY'S STATEMENT:

I celebrate, live, and discuss abundance.

Notes:

When Did You First Notice That: 92

The people who get the most money and who keep it the longest are the ones who understand the current "rules of the game.

TODAY'S STATEMENT:

I don't hide from what I need to know.

Notes:

When Did You First Notice That: [93]

If you think the world owes you a living, you will never have one.

TODAY'S STATEMENT:

I am grateful for everything I have.

Notes:

When Did You First Notice That: [94]

When we gamble, hoping that someday chance will make us rich, we do not realize that the habit of waiting has deprived us of one of our most precious commodities, time.

TODAY'S STATEMENT:

I know there is no need to gamble or wait when all that I need is present now.

Notes:

When Did You First Notice That: [95]

Some people think they are only rich if they have money.

TODAY'S STATEMENT:

I am rich because that is my natural state of being.

Notes:

When Did You First Notice That: [96]

Money is never the real motivation; it is what it represents.

TODAY'S STATEMENT:

I know what motivates me.

Notes:

When Did You First Notice That: [97]

If you spend more money than you make, you will not make a profit.

TODAY'S STATEMENT:

Wisdom guides my every action.

Notes:

When Did You First Notice That: [98]

Wisdom is far more valuable than money.

TODAY'S STATEMENT:

I Am Wisdom.

Notes:

When Did You First Notice That: [99]

Women not only need a "room of their own," they need an estate of their own.

TODAY'S STATEMENT:

My estate exists in the infinite.

Notes:

When Did You First Notice That: [100]

Everyone has a different version of "a lot" of money.

TODAY'S STATEMENT:

I am always deeply satisfied.

Notes:

OTHER DAILY NUDGE VOLUMES

Since *What You Perceive To Be Reality Magnifies*, imagine the outcome of taking **just 30 seconds a day** to become more aware and then consciously choosing what you are going to focus on for the day.

VOLUME ONE: 1-100

- In The Area Of Ourselves
- In The Area Of Communication
- In The Area Of Love
- In The Area Of Money

Volume Two: 101-200

- In The Area Of Others

- In The Area Of Groups And Partners

- In The Area Of Family

- In The Area Of Time

Volume Three: 201 - 300

- In The Area Of Choices

- In The Area Of World Affairs

- In The Area Of Pleasures

- In The Area Of How Life Works

Volume Four: 301 - 400

In The Area Of Travel

In The Area Of Beauty

In The Area Of Mortality

In The Area Of Purpose

Author Note

I started writing *The Daily Nudge* right after my first book, *The ABC's of Life From Women Who Learned The Hard Way*, came out in the early 1990s. I was in an advice frame of mind, noticing all the things I had never noticed before, and then writing affirmations for myself to counter my unawareness.

Of course, I also looked at people around me, and noticed what they didn't notice, and added those observations to my growing list.

This went on for a year during which I spent one month in New York City, in the World Trade Center (Yes, the one that was destroyed on 9/11) taking financial training classes with what became Morgan Stanley.

The speakers were only interesting enough to me to spark more ideas, and while they might have thought I was taking notes, I was mostly writing Daily Nudges. My room mate sat with me and laughed at me as I made one observation after another.

When I was ready, I showed it to my publisher who said, "That's not a book!"

A few years later, I pulled out my observations and turned them into a free email series. And then all these years later, I realized they could be a book. Not a "normal" book, but a journal type book.

And that's how these four volumes of *The Daily Nudge* were born. It was a long gestation period. But sometimes that's what it takes.

Thank you for giving these observations a chance to shift your life, as they continually shift mine. ~ Beca

Also By Beca

The Rivers of Time Series: Women's Lit, Friendship, Small Town, Mystery, Magical Realism, Small Town Fiction
The Returning, The Awakening, The Rising

Follow Me Here: **Women's Lit, Friendship, Small Town, Mystery, Magical Realism, Small Town Fiction**

The Ruby Sisters Series: Women's Lit, Friendship, Mystery, Small Town Fiction
A Last Gift, After All This Time, And Then She Remembered, As If It Was Real, Almost Innocent

Stories From Doveland: Women's Lit, Friendship, Small Town, Mystery, Magical Realism, Small Town Fiction
Karass, Pragma, Jatismar, Exousia, Stemma, Paragnosis, In-Between, Missing, Out Of Nowhere

The Return To Erda Series: Fantasy
Shatterskin, Deadsweep, Abbadon, The Experiment

The Chronicles of Thamon: Fantasy
Banished, Betrayed, Discovered, Wren's Story

The Shift Series: Spiritual Self-Help
Living in Grace: The Shift to Spiritual Perception
The Daily Shift: Daily Lessons From Love To Money
The 4 Essential Questions: Choosing Spiritually Healthy Habits
The 28 Day Shift To Wealth: A Daily Prosperity Plan
The Intent Course: Say Yes To What Moves You
Imagination Mastery: A Workbook For Shifting Your Reality
Right Thinking: A Thoughtful System for Healing
Perception Mastery: Seven Steps To Lasting Change
Blooming Your Life: How To Experience Consistent Happiness

Perception Parables: Very short stories
Love's Silent Sweet Secret: A Fable About Love
Golden Chains And Silver Cords: A Fable About Letting Go

Advice / Journals
A Woman's ABCs *of Life: Lessons in Love, Life, and Career from Those Who Learned The Hard Way*
The Daily Nudge(s): So When Did You First Notice

About Beca

Beca writes books she hopes will change people's perceptions of themselves and the world, and open possibilities to things and ideas that are waiting to be seen and experienced.

At sixteen, Beca founded her own dance studio. Later, she received a Master's Degree in Dance in Choreography from UCLA and founded the Harbinger Dance Theatre, a multimedia dance company, while continuing to run her dance school.

After graduating—to better support her three children—Beca switched to the sales field, where she worked as an employee and independent contractor in many industries, excelling in each while perfecting and teaching her Shift System and writing books.

She joined the financial industry in 1983 and became an Associate Vice President of Investments at a major stock brokerage firm. She was a licensed Certified Financial Planner for over twenty years.

This diversity, along with a variety of life challenges, helped fuel the desire to share what she's learned by writing and speaking, hoping it will make a difference in other people's lives.

Beca grew up in State College, PA, with the dream of becoming a dancer and then a writer. She carried that dream forward as she fulfilled a childhood wish by moving to Southern California in 1968. Beca told her family she would never move back to the cold.

After living there for thirty-one years, she met her husband, Delbert Lee Piper, Sr., at a retreat in Virginia, and everything changed. They decided to find a place they could call their own, which sent them off traveling around the United States. They lived and worked in a few different places before returning to live in the cold once again near Del's family in a small town in Northeast Ohio, not too far from State College.

When not working and teaching together, they love to visit and play with their combined family of eight children and five grandchildren, walk, read, study, do yoga or taiji, feed birds, and work in their garden.

www.ingramcontent.com/pod-product-compliance
Lightning Source LLC
Chambersburg PA
CBHW071900070526
44583CB00016B/1780